To/

★ VINTAGE ★

★ ★ ★

BORN IN
1975

★ ★ ★

Happy 50th Birthday

Take a trip back in time and discover everything you loved and maybe forgot about the 1970s.

Lots of love,

70s Child

Having been born in 1975, you witnessed the birth of new technologies that would change the world forever. You remember a world before technology invaded the everyday, unlike children born after the 90s. Having lived through a true childhood, you were able to play in the streets with your friends and make up games based on your imagination. There were many families who enjoyed a better standard of living than previous generations despite the social and economic unrest that characterized the decade. Consumerism grew as a result of families having more money to spend on leisure activities and products. There was a change in the fabric of society. Music and fashion are two of the most prominent examples of the move towards individualism. Amazing musicians and bands emerged during the 70s. The expansion of subcultures in society was accompanied by an explosion of new fashion styles. As a result of the divorce act passed in the late 1960s, the family structure began to change. One in eight families will be headed by a single parent by the end of the decade. Women's liberation is slowly gaining momentum. There is a growing number of women who stay in the workplace after getting married and having children. In society, there is a call for equality. Even so, when looking at advertising, it's clear that this was not achieved but rather was the seed of something greater. Taking a trip back to your childhood, this book revisits all those things you loved and knew as a child of the 70s.

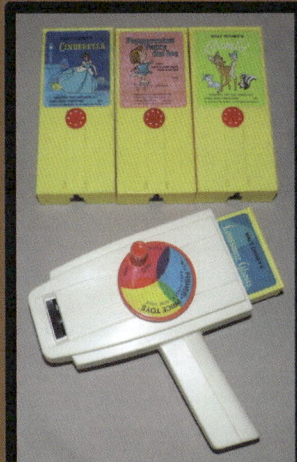

50 YEARS AGO BACK IN 1975

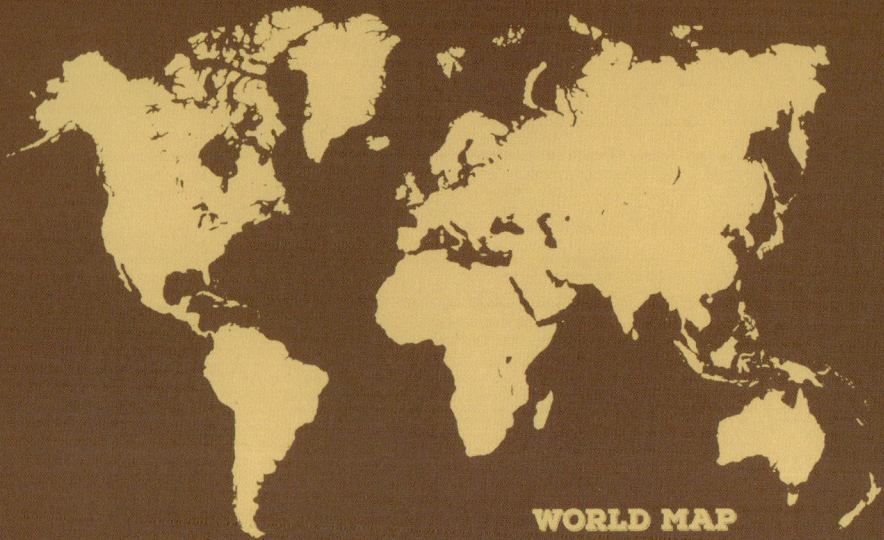

WORLD MAP

World Population

4 BILLION

Britain population

56.2 MILLION

2025

World Population

8.2 BILLION

Britain population

69 MILLION

MAJOR WORLD LEADERS

UK- PRIME MINISTER - JAMES HAROLD WILSON/MARGARET THATCHER

US PRESIDENT -GERALD FORD

RUSSIA/SOVIET UNION - FIRST SECRETARY OF THE CPSU LEONID BREZHNEV

SOUTH AFRICA - PRIME MINISTER - NICOLAAS JOHANNES DIEDERICHS

ITALY - PRIME MINISTER -ALDO MORO

WEST GERMANY - CHANCELLOR - HELMUT SCHMIDT

EAST GERMANY - ERICH HONECKER, CHAIRMAN OF THE COUNCIL OF STATE OF EAST GERMANY

FRANCE -PRIME MINISTER JACQUES CHIRAC

CANADA - PRIME MINISTER - PIERRE TRUDEAU

CHINA -PREMIER THE REPUBLIC OF CHINA -CHIANG CHING-KUO

PRESIDENT OF MEXICO - LUIS ECHEVERRÍA

You Have Been Loved for

50 YEARS

Thats 600 months

2609 weeks   18,262 days

438,291 hrs

26,297,460 MINUTES

1,576,800,000 seconds

and counting...

Cost of living 1975

Average House £9809

Average Salary £1809

Average gross weekly earnings of full-time manual men, aged 21 and over, in the United Kingdom were then £48.63. The corresponding figure for women manual workers, aged 18 and over, was £27.01

Average Car price

The Ford Cortina was the most popular car on the market in 1975, costing £1,840.

Cheddar cheese	40p	22" Ultra colour TV (Currys)	£259.00
Bread (white, 1¾lb.):		20" Ferguson black & white TV (Currys)	£74.95
wrapped and sliced loaf	15p	Daily Mirror newspaper	5p
unwrapped loaf	15p	½lb Lurpack butter (Safeway)	14p
white, 14oz. loaf	10p	Nescafé 4oz coffee (Tesco)	35p
brown, 14oz. loaf	10p	Can of coke (Tesco)7½p	49p
Flour, self-raising, per 3lb	20p	Indesit fridge-freezer (Currys)	£109.95
Milk, ordinary, per pint	6p	Hotpoint Supermatic twin tub washing machine (Currys)	£122.95
Sugar, granulated, per 2lb.	7.5		
Gallon of petrol 73p		Hoover Automatic Deluxe washing machine (Currys)	£145.95
Bottle of whisky (Haig)	£3.39		
Bottle of sherry (Harvey's Bristol Cream) £1.69		Golden Wonder crisps	8p
		One dozen large white eggs	38p
Watneys Party 4 (Peter Dominic)	85p	1lb Stork soft margarine	20p
Watneys Party 7 (Peter Dominic)	£1.35	Jacobs Cream Crackers (Sainsbury's)	13p
Pint of beer	28p	Stewed steak dinner at a transport cafe 40-50p	
20 cigarettes	42p		

Apollo-Soyuz Test Project

It wasn't the International Space Station that led to the first international partnership in space. It wasn't even the Shuttle-Mir series. This was the Apollo-Soyuz Test Project, the first international human spaceflight. A trio of Apollo astronauts launched on July 15, 1975, and docked with a pair of Soyuz astronauts two days later on July 17. An international rescue mission was the goal of the nine-day Apollo-Soyuz mission, which brought together two former rivals in spaceflight: the United States and the Soviet Union. On a Saturn IB rocket, the United States launched an Apollo command and service module. While nearly identical to the Apollo spacecraft orbiting the moon and carrying astronauts to Skylab, it was modified to provide for experiments, extra propellant tanks, and docking module controls and equipment.

It was on January 30, 1912, that Hungarian sculptor Ern Rubik applied for a patent for his "Magic Cube" invention, which is now known as a Rubik's Cube. Rubik studied sculpture and architecture at the Academy of Applied Arts and Design in Budapest, the son of a poet mother and a glider manufacturer father. He built geometric models as a hobby while working at the academy as a professor of design.

A woman becomes Prime Minister for the first time in 1975. Margaret Thatcher was elected as the new leader of the British Conservative Party. She won a landslide victory over four male candidates, she was the first woman to lead a British political party. Mrs Thatcher - who served as Secretary of State for Science and Education in Ted Heath's Government - exclaimed "It's like a dream."

Computer hobbyists Steve Wozniak and Steven Jobs begin developing computer designs. He and his friend Steve Wozniak built a prototype computer in his parents' garage. They develop the prototype Apple I in 1975. Apple Computer was founded just a year later to sell their machines.

Top Ten Baby Names

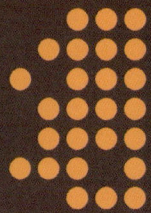

- SARAH
- CLAIRE
- NICOLA
- EMMA
- LISA
- JOANNE
- MICHELLE
- HELEN
- SAMANTHA
- KAREN

- PAUL
- MARK
- DAVID
- ANDREW
- RICHARD
- CHRISTOPHER
- JAMES
- SIMON
- MICHAEL
- MATTHEW

50 & famous

- Angelina Jolie - 4th June
- Christina Hendricks - 3rd May
- Kate Winslet - 5th October
- Bradley Cooper - 5th January
- David Beckham - 2nd May
- Charlize Theron - 7th August
- Enrique Englesias - 8th May
- Tobey Maquire - 27th June
- Drew Barrymore - 22nd February
- 50 Cent - 6th July
- Eva Longoria - 15th March
- Zach Braff - 6th April
- Alex Rodriguez - 27th July
- Cole Hauser - 22nd March

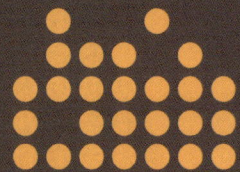

Music

Whenever you think of the 70s, you can't help but think of Glam Rock. Glam Rock provided an oasis of sparkle in an otherwise dreary, depressing political, social, and economic landscape. Elton John, David Bowie, and T-Rex are some of the icons of Glam music. There was an abundance of colour, style, and personality in the music of the 70s. Punk was also born during this revolt against the 'norm'. Sex Pistols, arguably the most well-known example of this, came later on in the 70s. The British music scene was awash with loud, diverse music scenes that refused to fade into the background.

1970 Edison Lighthouse

1971 T Rex

1972 The New Seekers

1973 Slade

1974 Abba

1975 David Bowie

1976 Abba

1977 Donna Summer

1978 Boomtown Rats

TOP POP HITS 1975

01	Bay City Rollers	Bye Bye Baby
02	Rod Stewart	Sailing
03	Windsor Davies & Don Estelle	Whispering Grass
04	Queen	Bohemian Rhapsody
05	Tammy Wynette	Stand By Your Man
06	The Stylistics	I Can't Give You Anything (But My Love)
07	David Essex	Hold Me Close
08	Art Garfunkel	I Only Have Eyes For You
09	Typically Tropical	Barbados
10	Johnny Nash	Tears On My Pillow
11	Bay City Rollers	Give A Little Love
12	10cc	I'm Not In Love
13	Roger Whittaker	The Last Farewell
14	David Bowie	Space Oddity
15	Pilot	January
16	Telly Savalas	If
17	Hot Chocolate	You Sexy Thing
18	Mud	Oh Boy
19	Steve Harley & Cockney Rebel	Make Me Smile (Come Up And See Me)
20	The Drifters	There Goes My First Love

Sir Roderick David Stewart CBE

Rod Stewart is one of the best-selling music artists of all time, having sold over 250 million records worldwide.

- 10 No.1 albums
- 31 top ten single hits
- 6 No.1 hits

He was knighted in the 2016 Birthday Honours for services to music and charity.

Marc Bolan; born Mark Feld; 30) died 1977

Marc had many strings to his bow but was most famously Lead singer of the band T.Rex and was one of the pioneers of glam rock.

SONY

VOLUME   TUNING

TUNING
FM

FM STEREO / FM·AM RECEIVER STR-7055 SOLID STATE

FM   88   90   92   94   96   98   100 102 104 106 108   MHz
AM   550   600   700   800   1000 1200 1400 1600   kHz

BALANCE

POWER HEADPHONE SPEAKER   BASS TONE TREBLE FILTER LOUDNESS MUTING MODE FUNCTION MONITOR AUX

The Supremes split in 1970, Ross then went from success to success spanning; a solo music career, television, film and stage performances. Ross' released her debut solo album that same year.

Everything Is Everything, gave her, her first UK number-one single "I'm Still Waiting".

She then dominated the world with her spectacular globe trotting sell out concert tours.

Albums - she enjoyed hit after hit with Touch Me in the Morning (1973), Mahogany (1975) and Diana Ross (1976) and their number-one hit singles, "Touch Me in the Morning", "Theme from Mahogany" and "Love Hangover", respectively. Ross further released numerous top-ten hits Throughout the 70s and into the decades that followed.

British rock group Mungo Jerry enjoyed success in the early 1970s, The group's name was inspired by the poem "Mungojerrie and Rumpleteazer", by T.S Elliot

Their biggest and most widely known hit was "In the Summertime".

TRANSPORT

The first Pan Am Boeing jet landed at Heathrow in 1970, kicking off the era of commercial flights. It was with that first flight that flying became more accessible to 'ordinary' families. All of a sudden, travel around the world became a realistic possibility, something most people couldn't imagine. Before this, British holidays were very much seaside trips or Butlins resorts if you were lucky. Changing technology influenced almost every aspect of life in the 1970s. The Concorde passenger aircraft, which is the fastest passenger aircraft in the world, was one of the most spectacular technological achievements of the 21st century. A real engineering feat, Concorde was built by Britain & France and first flew in 1976. At a speed of 2,100 kilometers per hour. 1976 to 2003 was the lifespan of Concorde. The airline's retirement was partly due to its extremely high fares, which were unaffordable for most people. Concorde flights between London and Washington originally cost £431 each. The number of cars on the road today is estimated to be 39 million. That number was closer to 13 million in 1971 or just a third of what it is today. Despite this, infrastructure growth has not kept pace. There were 246,700 miles of road in total in 2018, up less than a quarter from 203,400 miles in 1971.

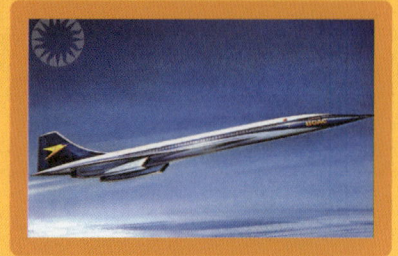

At the turn of the decade, the top four car manufacturers all released brand-new models. Ford Escort, which was launched in 1967, was one of the newer versions. As well as the Ford Capri, which is credited with bringing sports cars into the mainstream.

Top ten selling cars of the 70s

1. Ford Cortina
2. Ford Escort
3. Mini
4. Morris Marina
5. Vauxhall Viva
6. Austin/Morris 1100/1300
7. Austin Allegro
8. Ford Capri
9. Hillman Avenger
10. Austin Maxi

CHANGING TRENDS

Walking to work was the most common form of transportation between the 1890s and the 1930s and remained the main means of commuting for one-third to one-fifth of the population in small towns and cities as late as the 1970s. Bicycle use declined after 1950 as other forms of transportation became available. The decline continued until the mid-1970s when it levelled off, and usage has remained fairly consistent since then.

FORD ESCORT

From your Mercury deal

List : $8.50 (each kit) Plus tax   List : $7.80 (each kit) Plus tax   List : $26.00 each. Plus tax

e your Ford Dealer for these new accessory releases Ford

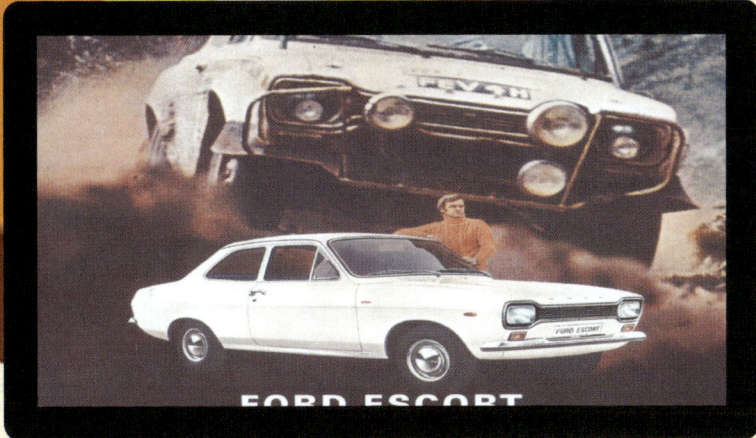

BRITISH LEYLAND build a car to suit your requirements. Check the model specification chart at the front of this booklet and see which car most nearly fits your own individual needs.

BRITISH LEYLAND ALSO PRODUCE A COMPLETE RANGE OF TRUCKS, BUSES, AUTOMOTIVE COMPONENTS, EARTHWORK AND CONSTRUCTION EQUIPMENT.

AUSTIN · DAIMLER · JAGUAR · MG · MINI · MORRIS · ROVER · TRIUMPH · WOLSELEY

Films

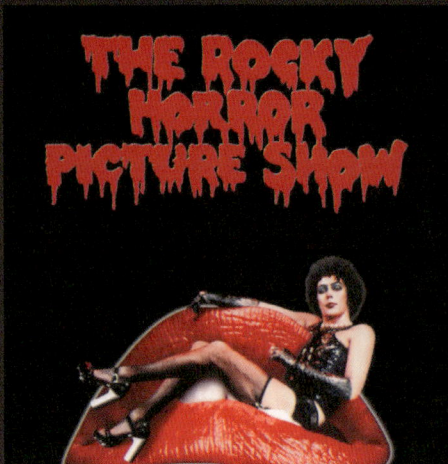

The Rocky Horror Picture Show

From October to December, shooting took place near Windsor, England, in Bray. According to Barry Bostwick, the castle was always leaking during filming. Cast members took turns warming up in one "warm room" filled with space heaters until the room caught fire.

Dog Day Afternoon

While Al Pacino initially agreed to play Sonny, he told Sidney Lumet near the start of production that he couldn't. He had just finished filming The Godfather Part II (1974) and was physically exhausted and depressed. Because he relied on the Method, Pacino did not relish the thought of working himself up to near hysteria every day. Dustin Hoffman received the script from Lumet after he unhappily accepted the actor's decision. After hearing that his rival was being considered for the role, Pacino changed his mind.

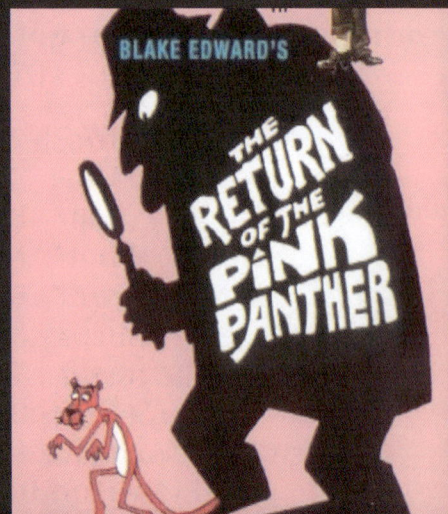

The Return of the Pink Panther

Lady Litton's (Catherine Schell's) laughter is mostly genuine. She had trouble keeping a straight face during many of her scenes with Peter Sellers (Inspector Jacques Clouseau). As a result, writer, producer, and director Blake Edwards decided to give up trying to get her to act the way she was supposed to.

Films 1975

- **Jaws** Universal
- **One Flew Over the Cuckoo's Nest**
- **The Rocky Horror Picture Show**
- **Shampoo** Columbia
- **Dog Day Afternoon** Warner Bros.
- **The Return of the Pink Panther** United Artists
- **Three Days of the Condor** Paramount
- **Funny Lady** Columbia
- **The Other Side of the Mountain** Universal
- **Tommy** Columbia

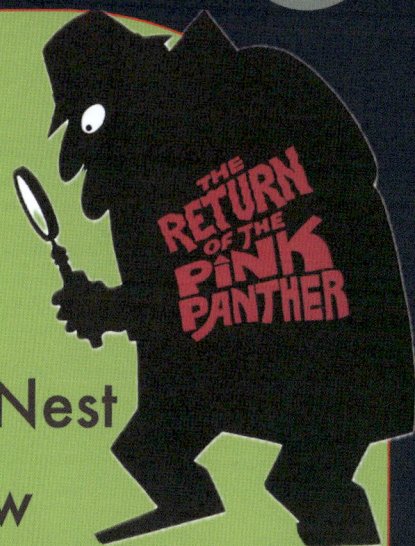

THE RETURN OF THE PINK PANTHER

Popular 70s TV Shows

In 1971, 91% of families owned a television

The early 1970s were characterised by a focus on comedy shows. Except for BBC's Steptoe and Son, ITV dominated this market. A great deal of progress was being made by the BBC toward assuming the comedy role by the mid-70s. 'The Good Life' (1975) and 'Faulty Towers' (1975) remain popular today. In the 70s, the BBC overtook ITV in producing the best and most popular shows on TV. Although you may have been too young to watch these shows at the time of their release, you will probably recognise some of those films. Today, many of these are still airing as repeats on television. Do you know what the big news of the decade is? Colour TV is available! Colour broadcasting began on 3 of the main stations by the end of the 1960s.

ARE YOU BEING SERVED?
UK (BBC) Situation Comedy. BBC 1 1973-9; 1981; 1983; 1985

ANTIQUES ROADSHOW UK (BBC) Antiques. BBC 1 1979-

ALL CREATURES GREAT AND SMALL
UK (BBC) Drama. BBC 1 1978-80; 1983; 1985;1988-90

THE BENNY HILL SHOW
UK (BBC) Comedy. BBC 1 1955-1968; Thames 1969-89

BLAKE'S 7 UK (BBC) Science Fiction. BBC 1 1978-81

BLESS THIS HOUSE
UK (Thames) Situation Comedy. ITV 1971-4, 1976

CALLAN UK (ABC/Thames) Secret Agent Drama. ITV 967-72

CILLA UK (BBC) Variety. BBC 1

CORONATION STREET
UK (Granada) Drama. ITV 1960-present day

CROSSROADS
UK (ATV/Central/Carlton) Drama. ITV 1964-88; ITV 1 2001-3

DAD'S ARMY UK (BBC) Situation Comedy. BBC 1 1968-77

DOCTOR WHO UK (BBC) Science Fiction. BBC 1 1963-89

THE DES O'CONNOR SHOW UK (ATV) Comedy.

FAWLTY TOWERS UK (BBC). Situation Comedy. BBC 2 1975; 1979

THE GENERATION GAME
UK (BBC) Game Show. BBC 1 1971-82; 1990- 2002

GEORGE AND MILDRED UK (Thames) Situation Comedy. ITV 1976-9

THE GOOD LIFE UK (BBC). Situation Comedy. BBC 1 1975-8

GRANGE HILL UK (BBC/Mersey). Children's Drama. BBC 1978-

LAST OF THE SUMMER WINE UK (BBC) Situation Comedy. BBC 1 1973; 1975-6; 1978-9; 1981-93; 1995-

PLEASE SIR! UK (LWT) Situation Comedy. ITV 1968-72

MORCAMBE AND WISE UK (ATV) Comedy. 1961-7; BBC 1 1968-76; ITV 978-84

MONTY PYTHON'S FLYING CIRCUS
UK (BBC) Comedy. BBC 1 1969-73; BBC 2 1973

OPPORTUNITY KNOCKS UK (Associated Rediffusion/ ABC/Thames/BBC) Talent Show. ITV 1956-78; BBC 1 1987-90

PRISONER: CELL BLOCK H
Australia (Grundy) Drama. ITV 1979-87

SOME MOTHERS DO 'AVE 'EM
UK (BBC) Situation Comedy. BBC 1 1973-5; 1978

STEPTOE AND SON
UK (BBC) Situation Comedy. BBC 1 1962-5; 1970; 1972-4

THE SWEENEY
UK (Euston Films/Thames) Police Drama. ITV 975-6; 1978

THIS IS YOUR LIFE UK (BBC/Thames) Entertainment. BBC

Adverts in the 70s

More houses than ever owned a colour TV with multiple channels during the 1970s. As a result, people had more choices than they had ever had before. This changed the way products were marketed, and brands were quick to take advantage of this new opportunity. Traditional advertising was done primarily in newspapers and magazines, but more brands were turning to television. It led to a consumer-based approach rather than the existing product-centric approach, giving consumers more control - if they didn't like the advertising they saw they switched over.

Although advertisements were still largely product-focused at the beginning of the decade, brands started digging deep into the narrative of why people should buy their brand over others as they recognised the importance of appealing to customers and communicating the reasons why their product was superior. Today, comparison ads are still seen in advertising as a result of this. A couple of obvious examples are Burger King versus McDonald's, and Pepsi versus Coke. Mothercare's advertisement on the following page shows another early example "See how much more your money buys at Mothercare..." showing not just the product benefits but how they compare to other brands. There were more rules & regulations in the 70s advertising world than in previous decades. Products no longer had the same elastic approach to listing their benefits. Regulations allowed for a more honest approach, which in turn increased consumer confidence. As you can see on the following page, PLJ lemon juice regulations weren't quite as strict as they are now. In short, this miracle juice will help you lose weight, look gorgeous, and have glowing skin. With the advancement of technology, companies were able to collect more information about their customers. For the first time, companies were gathering data to target their advertising. This included demographic information, analysis of consumer spending behaviour, and projections based on analysis of previous data. These were used in campaigns to increase demand for the brand/product. Ads are also increasingly emphasising emotional approaches. The result was advertisements we would now find offensive and would certainly not see on our televisions. A major culprit is sexual innuendo, a sign of how different cultures were just five decades ago.

Food brands and soap powder brands dominated TV ads in the 70s. The following double page features original 1970s ads. You might also remember the Smash Martians? Katie, who had appeared in OXO advertisements since the 1950s, travelled to America to tell her American friends about this wonderful cooking aid. As a result, the brand gained a sense of glamour. Originally made in 1903, HP Fruity Sauce is the original HP sauce. To offer a milder alternative to the original sauce, fruity sauce was developed in 1969. Are you aware that HP stands for Houses of Parliament? Frederick Gibson Garter, a Nottingham grocer, invented the original recipe. In order to settle a debt with Edwin Samson Moore of the Midlands vinegar company, he sold the recipe for £150.

Ad for Coffee Mate in a 1972 magazine. The product developed in 1961 was particularly popular throughout the 70s.

Joules Bel founded Babybel in 1865. With over 2 billion units sold worldwide, this long-established brand continues to be a success today

Ceylon tea and PG Tips- it wasn't until the 1970's that tea companies began selling tea bags instead of loose leaf tea. Although teabags were sold earlier in the century, they didn't catch on until the 1970s. This change in consumption was driven by advertising.

Old Spice's Christmas advertisement shows various gift sets. Your dad probably received a few of these along with some patterned socks during the 70's.

Vencat Curry Powder - curry was not popular before the 1970s. Due to the fact that most housewives were unfamiliar with the ingredient, the original ads provided recipe suggestions.

Hoover Gas fire, The Show-off- 1970 advert. The gas fire has been in households since the 1940s, but due to post-war austerity it was not commonplace until the 1960s, and even then it was used sparingly. With advertising, gas fires became increasingly popular in the 1970s as real coal fires became obsolete.

Wright's coal tar soap has been one of the most popular soaps in many homes since the 1860s. Even today, the soap can be used to treat various skin disorders.

Fashion 1970s

As the swinging Sixties gave way to the 1970s, fashion had become more accessible. There were multiple movements of the era reflected in the boutiques' individual styles. As new technologies emerged, the fashion industry was heavily impacted. It was mainly influenced by the availability of cheap fabrics through mass production. Polyester was embraced with wild abandon during the 70s, referred to as the 'Polyester decade'. At the time, it didn't seem to bother anyone that it was cheap and didn't allow any air to pass through. For both men and women, tight-fitted tops and wide bell-bottom trousers were typical silhouettes of the 70s. The family photo album may contain some spectacular flares with platform shoes!

It was the 1970s that saw a move toward individualism. There was a move away from the community spirit prevalent in the 1960s. Fashion influenced music, and music influenced fashion, allowing individuals to experiment with non-conformist styles. In mainstream society, we can see the beginnings of a much more casual approach to fashion. Are you familiar with the Peacock revolution? Although you would not have been old enough to participate, perhaps an older sibling or family member strutted around town in ruffled lacy shirts with lace on the cuffs and neckline. A sight to behold, hence the name Peacock Revolution.

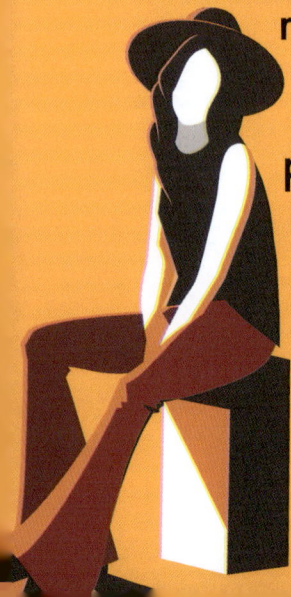

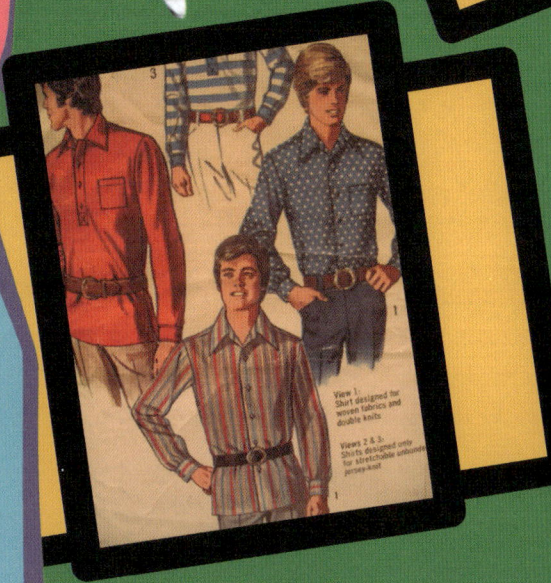

Designer Eyewear

Butterick 4139
$1.25
Canada $1.35

SIZE 28

1970s Fashion

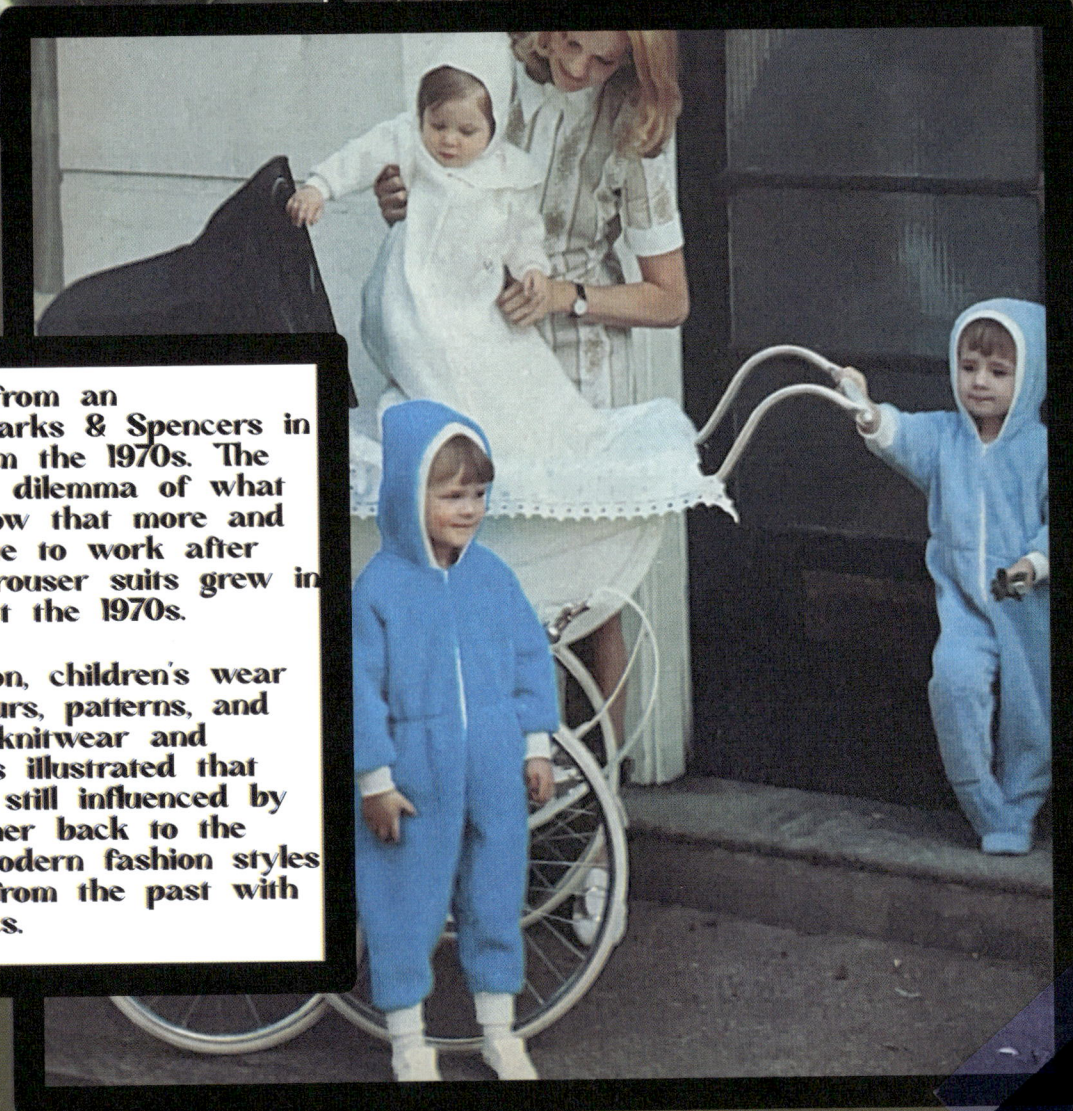

Images were taken from an advertisement for Marks & Spencers in Woman & Home from the 1970s. The article examines the dilemma of what to wear at work now that more and more women continue to work after marriage. Women's trouser suits grew in popularity throughout the 1970s.

As with adult fashion, children's wear followed bright colours, patterns, and stripes, as well as knitwear and crochet. The adverts illustrated that fashion styles were still influenced by the 1960s and further back to the 1930s and 1940s. Modern fashion styles incorporate details from the past with innovations in fabrics.

70s Toys

As a child of the '70s, you probably remember classics like Chopper bikes, roller skates, space hoppers, and the Atari computer. Let's reminisce about other 70's toys that were very popular.

Sindy doll wins 1970 Toy of the Year. Toys are sold in supermarkets. The neon Nerf Ball (costing £1.25) was the must-have Christmas toy. Katie Kopycat was named the 1971 Toy of the Year. We also witnessed the arrival of the Spacehopper and the beginning of the Clackers craze. The Mastermind board game cost a whopping £1.64 and was ranked number one on Santa's toy list.

The 1972 Plasticraft modelling kit won the coveted Toy of the Year award. A feature in Toy Trader forecasts the growth of leisuredromes - theme park shopping centres. The Uno card game (costs £1.01) is a Christmas must-have.

The retail awards introduced a new category, game of the year, won by Invicta's Mastermind. Plastic is in short supply due to industrial & economic issues, which is a problem for toy manufacturers. On average, children receive 9p in pocket money. Chelsea Girl and Daisy are brand-new dolls this year. A Christmas must-have is Shrinky Dinks; large sheets of pre-painted shapes or colours that shrink in a hot oven.

Star Wars !

In 1974, Lego won the Toy of the Year award for the first time. Trade is adversely affected by the 3-day week. Boxing toys Raving Bonkers, Denys Fisher Potter's Wheel, and the game Lexidata were among the biggest hits of the year. Fantasy tabletop role-playing game Dungeons & Dragons is a must-have for Christmas (costs £3.69).

1975 Lego wins again as Toy of the Year. The 40th anniversary of Monopoly is celebrated. Also celebrating a relatively young 25-year-old, Cluedo. Womblemania hits Britain. The theme tune might be familiar to you!

Game of Othello (costs £2.76) is a Christmas must-have.

In 1976, Peter Powell Kites won Toy of the Year as kites enjoyed a resurgence in popularity. Mattel set up shop in the UK 75 years after Meccano was invented. Streaker, a toy parodying yo-yos and hula hoops was the flop of the year. Christmas must-have toy - Magna Doodle (cost £2.63 - still available today).

The 1977 Toy of the Year award was given to Playpeople by Playmobil. This year's popular toys include slime, the Othello strategy board game, and Holly Hobbie. These Star Wars figurines cost £1.44 each and are a Christmas must-have.

The Combine Harvester made in Britain was the 1978 Toy of the Year. Huggy Bear is Chad Valley's first clinging bear. There is a new line of Star Wars toys on the market. Board and card games were launched by Omar Sharif at the NEC's Toy Fair. There were a number of big hits this year, such as Play-Doh Barber Shop - a childhood classic, Star Wars Force Beams, Matchbox Powertrack, and Mr. Men, as well as Skirrid, a new game that was a hit among adults and kids alike. Hungry Hippos (£3.94) was a Christmas must-have.

Do you remember?

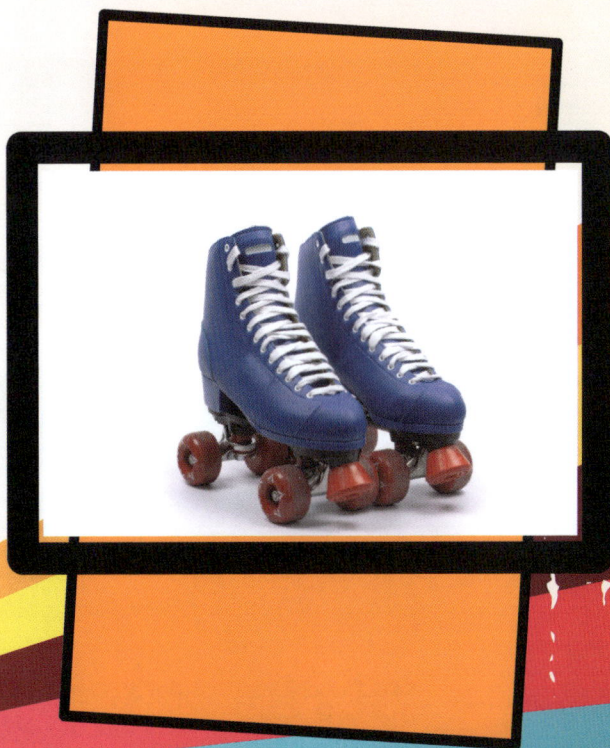

Popular 70s Children's TV shows

In 1968, Elisabeth Beresford created a series of books featuring furry creatures called the Wombles. A BBC-commissioned children's television show helped boost the characters' national profile in the UK in the mid-1970s. Stop-motion animation was used to create the series, which became an instant hit. The UK was hit by Womblemania and a number of spin-off novelty songs charted.

BBC Bristol produced Animal Magic, a kid's television series from 1962 to 1983. The show first aired fortnightly, then weekly in 1964.

A series originally made in black & white in 1958, Ivor the Engine enjoyed a revival in 1975 when new programmes were created using colour television

Playaway with Brian Cant. Cant, Brian (12 July 1933 - 19 June 2017). The programmes Playaway (1971–84) were hosted or co-hosted by Cant. From birth to the teen years, you'll surely remember this!

Originally shown on BBC's Blue Peter, Bleep and Booster is a children's cartoon series by William Timym. Between 1964 and 1977, 313 five-minute episodes were released.

David McKee created Mr. Benn in 1971. Red Knight was the first episode.

The BBC aired Crackerjack from 14 September 1955 until 21 December 1984 (except during the year 1971). It was a popular variety show for kids that lasted for four decades and was enjoyed by several generations.

Stop-motion animation children's television series The Clangers (BBC1 1969-1972). A small moon-like planet is home to a family of mouse-like creatures. They converse in a strange whistle-like language and are sustained by green soup and blue string pudding.

Do you remember?

Tiswas

Captain Pugwash

Rainbow

Basil Brush

Trumpton Fire Brigade

Roobarb & Custard

Bagpuss 13 episodes broadcast in 1974.

Banana Splits

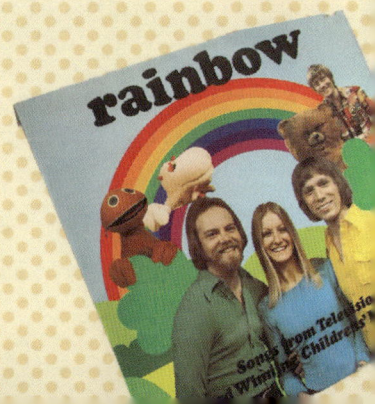

1975 UK Events

14th Jan - Donald Neilson kidnaps 17-year-old Lesley Whittle from her home near Bridgnorth in Shropshire, the daughter of the late bus operator George Whittle.

The Archbishop of Canterbury, Donald Coggan, is enthroned on 24 January.

20 Jan – The Channel Tunnel project is abandoned in 1974.

11th Feb - Conservative Party leader Margaret Thatcher defeats Edward Heath.

28th Feb - Moorgate station is hit by a major tube crash that kills 43 people.

4th Mar - Chaplin is knighted by Queen Elizabeth II.

The UK releases Monty Python and the Holy Grail on 3 April.

Led Zeppelin play five sold-out shows at Earls Court in London in May.

UEFA bans Leeds United from European competition for three years following the fans' behavior at the European Cup final.

5th Jun - Referendum results in a 'yes' vote for the United Kingdom to remain in the European Union.

British Leyland Motor Corporation is taken over by the British government on 11 August.

14th Aug - With a total rainfall of 169mm in just 155 minutes, Hampstead enters the UK Weather Records.

15th Aug - The Birmingham Six are wrongfully sentenced to life imprisonment for the Birmingham pub bombings.

1975 UK Events

The unemployment rate reaches 1,250,000 on 21 August.

The first British climbers reach the summit of Mount Everest on 24 September, led by Dougal Haston and Doug Scott.

The National Railway Museum opens in York on 27 September, becoming the first national museum outside London.

The Provisional Irish Republican Army bombs the London Hilton hotel on September 5th. There are two deaths and sixty-three injuries.

The first episode of BBC Two's popular sitcom Fawlty Towers airs on 19 Sep.

1st Oct - The "Thrilla in Manila" boxing match in the Philippines sees Muhammad Ali defeat Joe Frazier.

9th Oct - One person is killed and twenty others are injured in a bomb blast outside Green Park tube station near Piccadilly in London.

29th Oct With the murder of Wilma McCann, Peter Sutcliffe, otherwise known as the Yorkshire Ripper, commits his first murder.

3rd Nov - A petroleum pipeline opens from Cruden Bay in Scotland to Grangemouth.

25th Nov UK law outlaws the Irish Republican Army.

29th Nov - An aeroplane crashed during foggy conditions killing Formula One racer Graham Hill (b. 1929).

The Employment Protection Act provides for paid maternity leave, increases the jurisdiction of employment tribunals, establishes a Maternity Pay Fund, and prohibits unfair dismissals.

BBC One broadcasts The Wizard of Oz for the first time in Britain.

World Events

Leadership Contest

Feb 11 Margaret Thatcher defeats Edward Heath for leadership of the British Conservative Party

Everest is conquered by the first British climbers in 1975.

First Britons to summit Everest are Dougal Haston and Doug Scott. 33 days after setting up their base camp, the men reached the summit of Mount Everest via the previously unclimbed south-west face. This team set a record for the fastest time up the peak on a difficult direct route, which has repelled five other attempts. As a result of its length and exposure to high-level winds, the south-west face of Everest has been regarded as one of the most difficult challenges in mountaineering.

The Fall of Saigon

As the North Vietnamese forces advance, the US evacuates its citizens from Saigon in Operation Frequent Wind, ending US involvement in the conflict. Almost all American civilians and military personnel in Saigon were evacuated, along with tens of thousands of South Vietnamese civilians. Some Americans refused to evacuate. Ground combat units from the United States left South Vietnam more than two years prior to the fall of Saigon, so they were not available to assist with either the defense of Saigon or the evacuation. It was the largest helicopter evacuation in history.

The US conducts a nuclear test at the Nevada Test Site

Electoral corruption

Prime Minister Indira Gandhi is convicted of electoral corruption during her successful 1971 campaign. When public demonstrations threatened to topple her administration, Gandhi refused to resign and declared martial law in the country.

First World Cricket Cup

As the first major event in the history of One Day International cricket (ODI), the 1975 Cricket World Cup (officially called the Prudential Cup '75) was the inaugural men's Cricket World Cup. It was held between 7 June and 21 June 1975 in England, organized by the International Cricket Conference (ICC).

A total of eight countries participated in the tournament, sponsored by Prudential Assurance Company: Australia, England, India, New Zealand, Pakistan, and the West Indies, as well as Sri Lanka and East Africa, two of the world's leading Associate nations. In each group, four teams played each other once; the top two from each group qualified for the semi-finals, where the winners met in the final. It consisted of 60 overs per team, played in traditional white clothing and with red balls; all matches were played in daylight.

A 3,000-year-old monarchy is abolished in Ethiopia

Assasination of King Faisal

King Faisal is shot to death by his nephew, Prince Faisal, in Riyadh, Saudi Arabia. In the 1920s and '30s, King Faisal fought in military campaigns that helped shape modern Saudi Arabia. Following the ascension of his older brother, Saud, in 1953, he served as Saudi ambassador to the United Nations. When King Saud abdicated in 1964, Faisal became Saudi Arabia's absolute ruler. During his reign, he sought to modernize his nation and promoted anti-Israeli efforts in the Middle East. The throne of Saudi Arabia was inherited by Crown Prince Khalid after the assassination of Faisal in 1975.

Two thousand Led Zeppelin fans trash the Boston Garden

NBC premieres Wheel of Fortune on January 6, 1975, one of the longest-running syndicated game shows in American television history. Wheel is one of the most popular television shows in the world, created by television legend Merv Griffin and hosted by Pat Sajak and Vanna White since the early 1980s.

70s Inventions

1972

Hamilton introduces the world's first electronic digital wristwatch. The retail price is $2,100, which is over $12K in today's dollars.

1971 Floppy Disk

The first floppies were created by IBM engineers working on a reliable way to load instructions and data onto mainframe computers. In 1971, IBM began selling floppies. It wasn't until 1972 that they received a patent, and then Apple released their Apple II with a 5-inch floppy disk that their success began. Consequently, the general public was able to load programs and data onto their home PCs easily.

Blakenbaker invented what is widely considered the first personal computer while working at Kenbar Corporation in 1970. Early in 1971, Kenbak-I was released.

Sony Walkman
1979

It was this invention that shaped the culture of the 1980s. It revolutionized the way young people listen to music. The Walkman became an instant hit in 1979. A mixed tape on a walkman was a joy for many teenagers during the 80s.

When Intel released the 4004 microprocessor in 1971, it was the world's first microprocessor.

US President Barack Obama awarded the National Medal of Technology and Innovation to Stanley Mazor, Federico Faggin, and Ted Holff, co-inventors of the microprocessor.

70s Inventions

Rubix Cube

Designed by Erno Rubik (architecture professor) to teach spatial relationships to his students. The toy became one of the most popular toys of the 1980s. The challenge continues to be popular today!

In 1977, 3M launched a "Press 'n Peel" bookmark in four cities, but the results were disappointing. When the rollout introduction began in 1979, 3M instead issued free samples and rebranded its product as "Post-Its," which began to be sold across the country on April 6, 1980.

Early in 1971, Busicom released the pocket-sized electronic calculator LE-120A "HANDY".

An engineer at Kodak invented the first self-contained digital camera in 1975. Black and white photographs were taken with the camera created by Steven Sasson, which weighed 8lbs.

Mobile phones

Mobile phones are an essential part of modern day life. Martin Cooper, a Motorola senior engineer who invented the technology in 1973, is responsible for bringing this technology to life. Martin called a rival company (Bell Laboratories) just to let them know they were on a mobile phone. By today's standards, the first phones were enormous. Motorola Dyna weighed 2.5 pounds and measured 1/2 a foot in length. For a 30 minute call, it took 10 hours to charge.

Email 1971

As with mobile phones, emails have become an integral part of modern life. Email was sent for the first time in 1971. Through the ARPANET network, Ray Tomlinson and Bolt Beranek developed text-based technology that enabled messages to be routed through computers through the @ symbol.

There is some dispute over the true origin of the invention, however, as Shiva Ayyadurai claims to have invented an electronic messaging platform in 1978. He went on to receive the copyright for the invention of "email".

Britain in the 70s

It is widely reported that the 1970s were a time of hardship for many due to a struggling economy, strikes, the winter of discontent and general uncertainty that led to social and economic unrest. This decade was marked by constant strikes, primarily by postal workers, miners, and dustmen. In order to reduce electricity consumption, a three-day work week was imposed. To alleviate the shortages caused by the 1973.74 oil crisis, the Conservative government introduced this legislation. Electricity usage for commercial purposes was capped at 3 consecutive days on 1st January 1974, except for hospitals and supermarkets that were exempted. As inflation increased, wages did not rise in line with inflation costs, causing unions to suffer.

Throughout Britain, the Queen's Silver Jubilee was celebrated in 1977. Street parties were held across the nation to celebrate. During this time, many young people were growing dissatisfied with the legitimacy of the monarchy. In 1977, the Sex Pistols released the song 'God Save the Queen' to coincide with the Queen's silver jubilee. A rejection of the monarchy is evident in this song, which reflects the frustration with limited opportunities among young people.

Electing Margaret Thatcher as our first female Prime Minister made history. Despite the bleak picture this paints, and despite the fact that many people vividly recall the power cuts and scarcity of resources, the most shared memories are of happy childhoods, an ease of life that seems far from our technology-crazed world of today. It may just be nostalgia with some rose-tinted glasses thrown in for good measure. Childhood memories of Bagpuss, spacehoppers, and playing with your friends all day tell a story of an idyllic time. Despite the headlines, most ordinary families were doing better than ever.

The legal stuff...

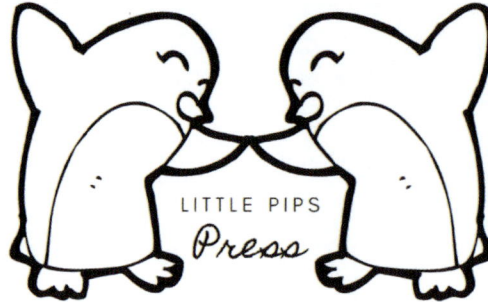

Attribution for photo images goes to the following talented photographers under the creative commons licenses specified:

Printed in Dunstable, United Kingdom